The Meaning of Home

JEFFREY ALAN MARKS

The Meaning of Home

Principal Photography by Douglas Friedman
Foreword by Suzanne Goin

RIZZOLI
NEW YORK

New York · Paris · London · Milan

CONTENTS

FOREWORD

INTERIOR DESIGN IS A VERY PERSONAL THING. IT'S LIKE STANDING in front of the world naked and saying, "Hey, everyone, this is me!" If it's successful, design excites, sings, and settles the soul. For me, the master of that harmony is Jeffrey Alan Marks.

As a Los Angeles restaurateur, I like to compare the design process to cooking. All the ingredients and materials in the world are available; the beauty is in how they are chosen, combined, and juxtaposed so the finished product becomes more than a sum of its parts. With the help of Jeffrey's design, my restaurants give diners something more than food: a comfortable atmosphere with an element of surprise. There's always something in his spaces that you wouldn't have thought would work but is all the more delightful for it. And color—the man is a master of color.

I first met Jeffrey in 2003, in my tiny bungalow tucked in Laurel Canyon. I had recently purchased the home and had just opened my first restaurant. Completely overwhelmed, I asked Jeffrey to help turn chaos into meaningful order. I was harping about natural, muted colors, elegant handmade materials, 1930s and '40s references, the Mediterranean, the garden, and God knows what else. My husband, David, freshly upgraded from his bachelor pad, was all about comfort and color. Oh, and we had no budget. Out of all of this, Jeffrey created what is still one of my favorite spaces: a perfect jewel of a dining room focused on a cozy banquette covered in rich yellow velvet. He gave me my Old World dining table and built a gorgeous modern display case for our treasures, which he painted the unexpected color of black. On either side of the banquette were the crowning glories of the room: bright orange étagères stuffed with our prized cookbooks. It was so JAM: luscious materials used in a playful way, creating a room that made us feel comfortable and very special at the same time. And yet the space was undeniably ours, a place that understood us perfectly. That little dining room makes me feel the same way I do when I taste a successful dish. It's a perfect combination of choices and tweaks, surprises and soulfulness.

Two homes and four restaurant designs later, I now give Jeffrey carte blanche on our projects together. He has not only helped draw out my personal, off-duty style but also reflected facets of my professional views of the dining experience that stand up as beautifully to a visiting U.S. president as to our beloved neighborhood patrons. Tavern is quietly stylish, elegant without being overpowering; the Hungry Cat is a comfortable, laid-back, contemporary beach house. Plans are on the table for our Montecito restaurant, which will have a midcentury, rustic hangout flavor.

Jeffrey's style never gets old because it's dynamic and incredibly livable. I can tell I'm in one of his spaces by the way good design, a sense of humor, and rich materials say, "Hey, this is me, and I like me!" He is constantly pushing himself in new directions, and I think that when you look through the pages in this book, you will see not only artful beauty in each space, but also a lovely balance. Our eyes and minds are delighted, but we are also centered and happy in Jeffrey Alan Marks's world.

—SUZANNE GOIN

INTRODUCTION

I AM NOT A MAN OF MANY WORDS. PEOPLE WHO KNOW ME FROM television may find that hard to believe, since on the show it looks as if I spend most of my day talking to people about design. But the reality is that I was daunted by the prospect of writing this book, because I am more comfortable communicating through my work. If you have stood speechless and in awe in front of Versailles or at the Richard Rogers' Lloyd's building in London, you know how great design can provoke an emotional response that words cannot sum up. Similarly, it's hard to explain how one room can make you feel one thing and another person feel something very different; nevertheless, a decorator knows instinctively how to assess a space for hidden potential, and how to put objects, fabrics, and colors together so that they are more than the sum of their parts. I think it's fair to say that designers can be abnormally fixated on how things look, and our minds tend to work more visually than verbally. But there is one part of the process—which is the core of my design philosophy—that does start with words: helping my clients discover what the meaning of home is to them. I strive to create rooms that are beautiful, of course—but far more important to me is that I create spaces that show the personal and unique meaning of home for each person, couple, and family that I work with.

I started my business at my kitchen table in a small flat on Eaton Place in London. Those early days, after design school, I modeled to support my design work, and for a few years, I spent more time modeling than designing. The advantage of this was that I got to travel extensively throughout the world, was exposed to great examples of architecture and design all over the continent, and even managed to pick up some decorating jobs along the way. My years abroad shaped and expanded my design sensibility, and to this day, they inform choices I make. I learned about subtlety from the French, color in Spain, comfort in England, and craftsmanship in Italy. Still, my love of California always tugged at my heart, and ultimately the pull westward was too great. After many years, I decided to return home and launch my business there.

While living abroad and constantly traveling for modeling jobs, I discovered a version of home that consists of a suitcase and a hotel room. I began bringing a candle wherever I went, so I could fall asleep to the same scent in Tokyo, Milan, or Paris—something I still do when I travel. In my tiny flat on Eaton Place, which was both my office and my living quarters, I became enthralled by the intimacy of small, functional spaces. Since then, I have always preferred tiny offices, because I know how much space I need to work, and who wants to be surrounded by square footage you don't need? When I moved back from Europe, my first home was on a golf course in La Jolla, and it was there I discovered how important it was for me to be able to look out on a beautiful, inspiring setting every day. Now, having a view is one thing that I know I cannot live without. In my current home, I brought in these influences from my past and combined them with other ideas for how I wanted to live. I love taking baths, and because of this, I made our bathroom a real living space, filling it with soft, upholstered furniture—and why not, because every human being on the planet spends more time in their bathroom than they ever will in their living room. As in many homes, our kitchen island is where guests always end up congregating, so I decided that it should be one of the most inviting spaces in the house. Mine is always decorated with bowls of beautiful fruit and vegetables from the farmers' market. During the week, we gather with friends around the island and feast on the glorious produce, which I complement with my culinary specialties: some good wine and wonderful cheese.

There is often a strong connection between someone's description of what home means to them and who that person is, personally, creatively, and professionally. One of my earliest clients was Mike Bruno, the founder of 1stdibs.com. When we first worked together twenty-five years ago, he described home as "a space where art, design, and nature blend happily and seamlessly"—a statement that could also describe the business he has gone on to create. My style mentor, fashion designer Brunello Cucinelli, tells me his idea of home is embedded in his past: "It's the essence of our origins, the paths we've walked, a reminder of our work that provides a daily

drive to move forward." Brunello lives and works in the village of Solomeo, Italy, where he has created a home, a clothing company, and a lifestyle that does exactly this: he moves forward with an eye to the strong traditions of Umbria and a vivid connection to his Italian heritage. My friend and client Amber Valletta says her home "is a sacred space that holds my dreams, inspires my creativity, gives my family comfort, and is a place where I can be just as I am." It makes sense that someone in the public eye, who spends her days giving so much of herself to the camera, would want a home that is a sanctuary and that refuels her creativity.

In my work, I see truth to the old adage "beauty is in the eye of the beholder" every day. Each of my clients has his or her own style and requirements for a home, and one of the things I love most about my job is working with such strong, distinctive individuals. In the pages ahead, you will see a Belgian-influenced Malibu family home; a sand-strewn beach house in Nantucket; an unbuttoned, bohemian flat in a beautiful London neighborhood; and an urban ranch in Austin, whose owners prize their family's laid-back comfort as much as they do their beloved collection of contemporary art. Whether grand or breezy, colorful or formal, the one thing these spaces have in common is that they reflect the personalities, pasts, and ways of life of the people that live in them. I take pride in the fact that these spaces are more about them than me.

One of the greatest lessons I've learned in my career is that to create a really outstanding, satisfying home, you need to throw out the rule book. Rules were meant to be broken. Rather than looking at a space and trying to figure out how I can add square footage, increase resale value, or incorporate a gym or media room or whatever other dedicated space happens to be in vogue, when working with people I try to figure out what they really need. If you're an outdoorsman who never spends time in a gym, why build one? If you've been living comfortably in a certain amount of space, why strive for more? And if you build a home that you love living in—one that reflects your tastes and habits and renews your spirit—you won't care as much about the resale value anymore. I hope this book inspires you to discover what home means for yourself—and gives you the courage to express it.

Breezy

Interiors characterized by a relaxed, "breezy" quality are probably the type I'm most associated with. As a native Californian, there's a certain amount of lightness cruising through my DNA, and a laid-back point of view is an intrinsic component of my work. Whether I'm designing a London townhouse, a New York apartment, or a cottage in Laguna Beach, I believe in maximizing comfort and try to create casual, friendly atmospheres that beg to be lived in. To me, "breeziness" is more of a state of mind than a geographic condition: its openness and a quality that makes spaces feel welcome for both owners and guests. One of my mantras is that every room in your home should be used daily—the days of holding your living room hostage for company are over.

A rusted nineteenth-century anchor propped up by the entry porch sets a leisurely tone for a Malibu home.

Santa Monica Canyon
California

MY HOME IS LOCATED ON A HILLSIDE IN SANTA MONICA CANYON. I bought the property because it has the best views of the ocean and is located on my favorite street. But the house itself had no charm, style, or sophistication whatsoever. As a matter of fact, it was the worst house on the street—which is partly why I fell in love with it. It was a home in my dream setting that I could make all my own. My partner, Ross Cassidy, and I live and work together, so creating a house that felt like home to both of us was an interesting challenge. We shared similar objectives: make the most of the views; keep it casual, comfortable, and dog friendly; and most importantly, make it feel welcoming to all who come inside. Ross is South African, and his tastes tend to be quite contemporary. I'm an American and more of a traditionalist. We both love the beach and anything nautical. We both favor a palette of blues and greens. So my design process was less about meeting in the middle than working with the things we had in common and accenting them with a playful contrast between our individual tastes. Our house is our design lab. I am always experimenting with new decorating ideas and inflicting different fabrics, paint colors, accessories, and art on its patient, understanding rooms. Our friends often remark that they never know what to expect when they walk through the French doors—even if they were just around for dinner last week. I'm happy to take risks in my own home, and I find that it helps me avoid unexpected outcomes in my clients' houses. A wonderful architect I once worked with said that there's a reason why our profession is called a design *practice*. I approach my work as constant practice—a fun, playful practice—and Ross and I are my most willing test subjects. Our small, constantly evolving canyon home shows off my design sensibility more than any finished product since it's where I can always express myself freely.

The stairway leading to my dressing room functions as a gallery, with art I've collected over the years hung salon style and interspersed with some of Ross's paintings. A rope handrail is a nod to the beach and a reminder that the ocean is never far from our thoughts.

I can't help myself. I
love including a playful
element in a design scheme
whenever I possibly can.
It's a professional tic.
I had yearned to use this
sea turtle rug for years,
but could never convince
a client to go for it.
So I finally just put it
in my own home and I
couldn't be happier with
it. It's the glue that binds
all the disparate elements
of the room together.

The living room is Exhibit A of the design laboratory that we call our home. A Christopher Farr rug with a turtle motif, which I had custom colored, defines the room. It is made of knotted silk and wool, which creates a blend of textures. I like to experiment with polar opposites, and here I placed a modern white chair across from a black antique wing-back chair for a happy collision of styles. The painting above the fireplace felt too formal, so I ripped it out of its frame. The coffee table is 1970s Italian, and I designed the turned wooden side table for an old house of mine. Over the years, it's been painted every color of the rainbow, but right now it's wire-brushed and dragged with white paint. The nickel floor lamp is from Galerie des Lampes in Paris, and the small gray pedestal pot is made of sun-dried clay from the 1600s. The vase is actually a wooden cog from the 1840s. It's filled with chamomile, broccoli, and celery root. I'm not a big fan of formal flower arrangements—we do most of our flower shopping in the fresh produce aisle.

YOUTH AND BEAUTY
ART OF THE AMERICAN TWENTIES

TRA

I placed my old industrial English desk in front of the window so I could stare at the bamboo garden and daydream. The chair is an old French flea-market find. It was falling apart so I had it reconditioned and upholstered in green silk velvet with a lavender trim, which matches nothing else in the room and works all the better for it. The lamp is one of the first antiques I ever bought. The base started its life as part of a piece of architecture in England. It's had over twenty different shades in the course of its time as a lamp, and this incarnation is my friend Peter Dunham's paisley. I'm an informal collector of antique boxes, and the specimens I've gathered over the years include this reeded ivory box with bun feet and the metal safe-deposit box from a defunct Swiss bank, which is now filled with love letters.

ABOVE: There's nothing I love more than a built-in window seat. I nestled this one between two bookshelves. The seat cushion is overstuffed with goose down and not as attractive as it would be if it were more tailored, but far more comfortable this way. One of my design tenets is that one can never have enough pillows. The yellow alpaca bolsters used here serve a dual purpose of comfort and color. I really could not afford the black ink painting from the early 1800s, but a friend, the late antiques dealer Amy Perlin, forced me to buy it from her and I don't regret it. It's the only piece I personally own from her now-shuttered store, which every decorator in America misses.

OPPOSITE: I like to put a comfy chair alongside a desk so that someone can come chat with you while you work. And when the workday is over, the tripod table is the perfect spot on which to set a drink. The yellow glass vase is American from the 1920s, and the painting shows a hedge on the drive I used to live on in La Jolla. The hodgepodge of art and mementoes along the wall includes a photograph of my dad, abstract paintings by Ross and Sara Eichner, and a collage by Tony Brown.

I designed our open-plan dining room and kitchen to face the windows and take full advantage of the property's spectacular ocean views. The French oak is hand waxed to achieve the perfect level of gloss. I stained the oak floors to match the hair of my blonde Labrador, Chessie, who sheds terribly. I designed the dining table and had it finished in a weathered blue to match the rowboat that hangs from the ceiling in my bedroom, the house's signature piece of furniture. Richard Wrightman and I customized the dining chairs, and the bar stools are from my furniture collection with Palecek. Simple nickel pendant lights over the island are reproductions of old factory lighting. The ceramic vases on the dining table were a gift from my dear friend, fellow decorator, and *Million Dollar Decorators* cast mate Kathryn M. Ireland. I love the way the sea-grass limestone countertop on the island, the stainless-steel counter, and zinc-edged backsplash contrast with the wood in the kitchen. They add a touch of industrial strength to a traditional scheme.

ABOVE: My favorite wallpaper of all time is de Gournay's hand-painted fish. This aquatic design has become my trademark. In my home, the school swims in the direction of the Pacific Ocean. The paper itself is silver, which has oxidized over time to develop a lovely dull tone—it's also a perfect symbol for the constantly evolving quality of this home. We pile up the island with whatever is fresh at the farmers' market; green figs and watercress were in season on this particular day. The hundred-year-old butcher block is a perfect thickness and size for chopping, cutting, and displaying.

OPPOSITE: My butler's pantry is lacquered in bright green. Ross insisted the countertop be African soapstone, as it reminds him of his native South Africa. An Angelo Mangiarotti light sits on a silver tray and reflects into the room. I intentionally designed the room to be very dark to create a perpetual party atmosphere.

CLOCKWISE FROM TOP LEFT: My objective in designing is to create a space that makes the inhabiter happy—the vintage Abercrombie & Fitch rowboat that hangs from our bedroom ceiling does just that for me. This room is not light on bold gestures. The massive clockface comes from an old train station in Pennsylvania. I backlit it so it serves as a giant night-light. The lamps are 1940s American. The carpet is blue and green, my favorite colors; I had it custom-made because I was unable to track down the perfect combination stripe. All the furniture is my own design. The color scheme is based on one of my favorite fabrics, Carnivale, which I used to upholster the bench at the foot of the bed. It took a lot of restraint on my part not to upholster the walls in the same fabric. Instead, I chose a simple hand-printed indigo block print from India. It has faded dramatically over the years to what I think is the perfect washed-out, beachy blue. I always have a few extra ottomans around. They help layer a room, and you can pile books on them. Ross could not live without Frédérique Morrel's sculpture of a raccoon with needlepoint skin and a real raccoon tail.

31

Our dressing room cabinets are a deep, washed-out gray. Gray is a perennial in fashion, and no matter how much I change the rest of the house, this room will stay that color forever because it's a great color in which to check out an outfit—it never clashes with what you are wearing. The silver bouillotte lamps were one of the biggest splurges in the house but well worth the money, as I admire them every day. The fish that swallowed the ship is also a lamp, and it is the perfect kitsch counterpoint to the seriously tasteful bouillottes.

ABOVE: I am probably the world's biggest proselytizer for putting comfortable furniture in a bathroom. I upholstered this high-back sofa in terry cloth so you can sit on it when you are wet. The walls are papered in grass cloth, which is not the most obvious choice for a wet room, but it actually holds up well and adds a lot of texture.

OPPOSITE: I like bathrooms that don't look like bathrooms, which is why I designed the vanity like a real piece of furniture. I had the freestanding double-sided mirror fabricated in France. Standing the vanity in the middle of the room, rather than having the ubiquitous pair of sinks shoved against a wall, is more attractive and more convenient. It allows us both to get ready at the same time without crowding each other. A chaise upholstered in Chelsea Editions linen is the perfect spot to relax in after a hot bath.

BASQUIAT
TONY SHAFRAZI GALLERY

Seaside Interiors

LIVING ARCHITECTURE

THE HAMPTONS

CASA MEXICANA STYLE

COLACELLO'S OUT

FORGOTTEN MODERN California Houses 1940–1970

STABLES Modern Spaces for Horses

The Gardens of Luciano Giubbilei

LIVING WITH WINE

PREVIOUS SPREAD: We found the footlocker that we use as a coffee table at Garden Court Antiques in San Francisco. The sofa is loaded with pillows of all sizes, shapes, and colors, further evidence of my belief that more is more when it comes to pillows. The chair is loosely upholstered in a scarf printed with a map of the world, and the shelf unit was salvaged from an old Los Angeles factory. The walls are painted Farrow & Ball Green Blue.

RIGHT: The sunroom off our bedroom has uninterrupted windows on all three walls, providing views of the ocean. It has the best natural light in the house, which is why Ross uses it as his painting studio. This does not thrill me or my custom-made striped carpet, but the collection of silver tea caddies makes the mess seem prettier, and there's a spiked baseball bat by the artist Sage Vaughn to remind the paint to keep itself in line. A deep window seat behind the table spans the width of the room and is upholstered in a fresh Loro Piana lilac cotton.

Malibu
California

THIS IS ONE OF MY FAVORITE KINDS OF SPACES: A COMFORTABLE home that highlights the personality and family dynamic of its inhabitants without losing a sense of its surroundings, which in this case is the sunny, outdoorsy essence of Malibu. The stunning garden, sweeping views of the Santa Monica mountains, and East Coast architecture all share focus with the spirit of the beach, which is just a short walk away. The clients are a European family, equipped with worldly taste and exceptionally green thumbs. Inside, textiles from Japan, Africa, and Belgium and Swedish and English antiques give a cosmopolitan sensibility that is perfectly tempered by a beach-inspired palette of blues, browns, and neutrals. The clients are passionate collectors of vintage and collector-quality cars, and it was very important to them to create a special space at the entrance to the home where they could display examples from their prized collection. The driveway was designed to serve as both an entryway and a viewing gallery for the cars. Its forecourt, also filled with lush greenery, leads into the main garden space, blending two of the clients' great passions into the home before you even get to the front door. The garden, the real star of the property, is the heart of the home, and all the rooms open onto it through a series of French doors.

The interiors were designed to be unfussy and comfortable. The artful mix of furniture and accessories from different design periods and far-flung locales share one common thread: a weathered quality that suggests loving and regular use. These furnishings help articulate the sense that every piece of this home, both inside and outside, is cherished and lived in.

An assemblage of weathered, crumbling, and unfussy objects gives this space a more welcoming feeling. The Gustavian chair retains its original torn upholstery and coir stuffing. The saddle is by Hermès, and the leather-bound antique books in a messy pile are from a Paris flea market. The French carved-oak game table has been stripped of its varnish; the dry wood adds a well-worn air that complements the rest of the tableau. A tiny etching fills a gap on the paneled wall.

ABOVE: The clients wanted a forecourt to display vehicles from their collection of vintage cars, so we built this stone path as an extension of the garden. A shiny black Porsche speedster was the inspiration for the black pots and gleaming lacquer on the front door. Matching metal benches, one with a woven cane top, help make the space intimate and comfortable— two qualities not usually associated with a driveway.

OPPOSITE: The entry hall scheme was designed around this abstract painting from the clients' art collection. A runner from Mansour was chosen to modernize the room. The Swedish secretaire, which I paired with the Gustavian hall chair, is from the early nineteenth century. To keep the room from feeling too formal, I introduced a comical rusted cast-iron sculpture, which sits on the floor next to the desk, and a ceramic vase by Antoinette Faragallah.

ABOVE: In the dining room, a traditional walnut table holds court between two eras of Italian furnishings. The vintage black dining chairs with leather backs and seats are from the 1930s; the painted bench is from the 1840s. I rounded out the time travel with a contemporary flat-weave rug from Mansour and used seventeenth-century Spanish signal cannons as candleholders, because why not?

OPPOSITE: In the living room, a 1940s sofa by Danish designer Kaare Klint sits next to a John Dickinson plaster coffee table. All the pillows are made from salvaged vintage Japanese fabrics. The green leather chair is vintage English. The rug in the foreground is contemporary, and the rug in the second seating arrangement is Swedish Deco. This room is an amalgam of styles and periods, which is typical of my aesthetic; I love trying to create a cohesive look out of improbable unions.

ABOVE: Antique stone vessels brimming with lemons and limes provide the JAM-allowed minimum of color in a white-on-white kitchen. The plaster sheep's head brings a requisite touch of humor.

OPPOSITE: I often design kitchens that are more subdued than the rest of the house; but even so, this monochromatic kitchen was an exercise in restraint for me. The white-on-white story is brought to life by the dramatic light fixture, which is a conglomeration of found objects. The barstools add a hint of rustic visual stimulation. Open shelves are much easier to use than closed cabinets, but they need to be consciously styled. In this instance, white dinner plates and bowls are perfect for a big family whose members are constantly grabbing whenever they please.

ABOVE: This outdoor dining room is often used for entertaining, so my goal was to make it as comfortable as possible for alfresco meals. French cast-iron lanterns hang from old ship pulleys on the stone loggia to provide light, and firewood storage under the cement counters is handy to feed the fire on chilly evenings.

OPPOSITE: I couldn't design an all-white kitchen without the promise of some color in the breakfast nook. Here, I layered a hand-woven Swedish Deco rug over jute matting to create a colorful seating arrangement. The table is early American, probably circa 1800. The clients are European and passionate about homegrown food. The produce on the table is from their kitchen garden.

ABOVE: Landscape architect Scott Shrader designed a series of outdoor "rooms" for the garden, including this shaded cement and gravel pathway that leads through a grove of trees to the tennis court. A pair of antique lead swans gives the walkway a touch of *Alice in Wonderland*-style fantasy.

OPPOSITE: I put these sculptural webbed-rope rocking chairs from Blackman Cruz around the swimming pool to liven up a traditional poolside seating area.

ABOVE: Around the fire pit outside the guest house, I dressed up the built-in stone "sofa" with throw pillows made of vintage tribal and Japanese textiles. The two striking metal and wood Cleo Baldon campaign-style armchairs are upholstered with removable leather cushions.

OPPOSITE: A pergola covered in flowering vines provides shade for an outdoor dining room. I played with the family's Euro-American mix by pairing weathered antique Gustavian chairs and a very long, painted Gustavian farm table with heavy, rustic American sliced-log chairs. In keeping with the idea of breezy comfort, all of the furniture I used here is already well-worn, so the family doesn't have to feel guilty about leaving it outdoors. Primitive wooden bowls from Belgium, a ceramic dish by Danish potter Arne Bang, a stone ball, and spiky metal stars round out the appropriately international mix.

TAILORED

I think that my role as a designer is similar to that of a tailor. Where he cuts a garment to the particular specifications of each customer's body, I try to fit each home I design as specifically as I can to its owner's personality. My clients come from a wide range of backgrounds, and there's no common thread of taste, career, or lifestyle. This makes my work exciting, and I feel privileged to have clients who don't want to rely on a template and always allow me to custom fit a design to them as individuals. To me, living in a tailored way is about individuality and harmony. The unique homes in this chapter show how the personalities of each of my wonderful clients become the inspiration for comfortable designs that fit each family to a T.

An ornate Claude Lalanne crocodile bench takes center stage in front of the fireplace in this Austin family home. The chairs are upholstered in real zebra hides; their manes make a perfect fringe. The decorative mirror and sconces are from the clients' collection of exquisite antiques.

Austin
Texas

THIS FAMILY HOME IN TEXAS IS OWNED BY DEAR FRIENDS OF OURS. Their architect, Michael Landrum, designed a house so perfectly proportioned and wonderfully detailed that decorating was a breeze. The couple collects art, and they are design enthusiasts; in their design brief, no idea was off limits. So I got to use every crayon in the box, and they had enough trust to let me experiment with things that might not have made sense on paper but paid off visually in the end. The result is a house that is a complex blend of formal and casual, a mix dictated in part by the three children who roam the fine-art-filled rooms. My clients believe, as I do, that spaces are meant to be lived in, not just looked at. I feel that you only see the real character of a home once people have relaxed in it: when the down fill in a sofa cushion settles into the shape of the bodies that have sat on it; when sheets soften after repeated laundering; and when the sweet smells of family cooking start to seep into the walls. A house is not a home until it has a stain or two on the sofa!

Inasmuch as this is a family home, it is also a showcase of the distinctive style of its owners. They have a passion for the exotic and unconventional. Animal hides abound, and mounted hunting trophies are as prolific as artwork. The collection of Lalanne furniture brings together their love of art, design, and the wild. For me, the most interesting aspect of the house is how the traditional Spanish design of the home becomes the perfect foundation on which to highlight their unique collection of objects, art, and furniture. This home's meaning comes from the combination of all of its roles: it's a family home, a gallery, an explorers club, and a playground.

The library was designed to feel like an old explorers club, full of references to far-flung destinations. The ornately carved table is from the Far East, the silver tray table is Indian, the antique rug is from the Middle East, the dazzling pendant light with orange glass panes is Moroccan, and the iron sconces are from Mexico. I rounded out the global tour with zebra hides, rattlesnake skins, and a trophy mounted above the antique Italian fireplace.

ABOVE (LEFT and RIGHT): The entry hall floor tiles are terra-cotta that has been lacquered black. The drama of the contrast between the black floors and vast white walls sets a dramatic tone for what's to come in the rest of the house. A tin rhinoceros by Sergio Bustamante stands defiantly on an ornately carved Spanish console. The massive black-and-white artwork is by Retna. Groupings create visually entertaining ways to punctuate ordinary spaces. A collection of stacked orange boxes and a series of star-shaped lanterns give this hallway a pleasantly off-kilter vibe. The orange leather upholstery on the custom-made bench completes the experience.

OPPOSITE: My clients are avid art collectors. Here, a portrait by Diego Rivera hangs above a Lalanne crocodile console. Over the antique chest of drawers is an abstract painting by Julian Schnabel.

OVERLEAF: I designed the gilded branch console in the foreground with a local artist to add a homegrown note of whimsy to a room that packs plenty of colorful, lighthearted references. In the spirit of unexpected touches, we turned the rug upside down because the colors were richer on the reverse side, and the texture felt less formal. I reupholstered the orange lacquered chinoiserie chairs in a loud blue-and-cream-patterned velvet, which complements the cream silk velvet sofas. Pillows made from axis hide, Fortuny cotton, cashmere, and a simple linen stripe liven up the neutral sofas.

In the dining room, a gold-glazed ceramic antler chandelier by Jason Miller imparts some rock-and-roll glamour to the earthy tones on the wall. The pink chairs and bright blue graffiti artwork by Retna play off the serious tone set by the massive eighteenth-century sacristy cabinet. On top of the cabinet sits a pair of carved-stone mythical beasts. They were originally architectural details on a building, and I love the lively attitude they bring to the room. The painting above the fireplace is a study by Diego Rivera.

ABOVE: I've never been a fan of rooms that serve only one purpose. The addition of a dining table and really comfortable chairs make this wine room much more usable. The room is refrigerated to the optimal temperature for keeping the wine, which is not, of course, the optimal temperature for dinner guests, so we put thick wool Hermès blankets on top of every chair. In the middle of a hot Texas summer, this is the best place to cool off.

OPPOSITE: A well-stocked bar is hidden behind antique doors in the living room.

OVERLEAF: I often use the kitchen as a palette cleanser for rest of the house. Simplicity wins in a room that has to meet the multitude of demands from residents large and small. Next to the kitchen is the butler's pantry where a neon sign by Ben Livingston has been installed. With the flick of a switch from the dining room, help is on the way.

Moorish motifs are nothing new to Mediterranean architecture. I love them most when they are incorporated into a design scheme in subtle ways. The terracotta floor tiles in this home are a Moroccan staple, and I used them in two very different ways. Left in their natural state outside they have weathered beautifully over time. Indoors they are painted a deep inky black, making them the perfect backdrop to showcase this home's sculptural furniture.

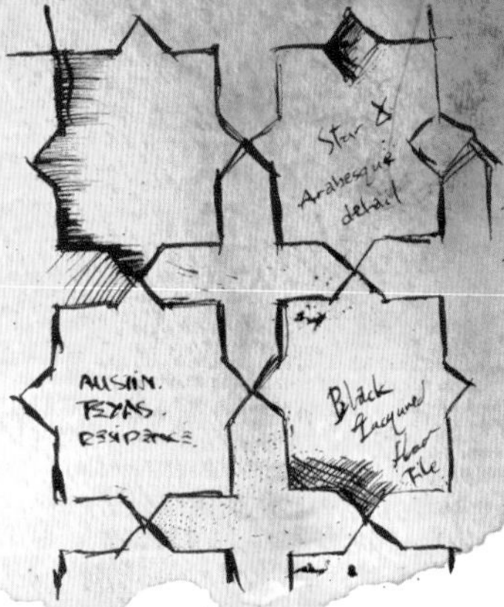

Star & Arabesque detail

AUSTIN, TEXAS. ESTATE.

Black Enamel Floor Tile

OPPOSITE: As a designer, I feel lucky to have been born a Libra, so that looking for balance is completely ingrained in me. To avoid pattern overkill here, I mixed a cabana stripe with a more subdued solid fabric on the sofa. The heavy carved table is African, and the painted flowerpots are from Mexico.

San Francisco
California

THIS SAN FRANCISCO APARTMENT WAS BUILT IN THE LATE 1920S. After my clients purchased it, we were given six months to do a complete renovation, a task I would undertake only for these beloved clients because we had successfully completed two other homes for them, and our working relationship was already familiar and comfortable. At some point in the apartment's eighty-year life, it had been renovated, and its original floor plan had been turned into something mazelike and awkward. We tore it down to the studs, keeping only the plaster moldings wherever it was possible. We researched the history of the building and found the plans from the 1920s, and so we returned many of the spaces to their original period style. When updating rooms with modern amenities (such as in the bathrooms and kitchen), we were respectful of the apartment's original spirit. During demolition, we discovered windows in the living room that had been closed up for forty years; we opened them up and incorporated them into the new design. The unobstructed views of the Golden Gate Bridge through this trio of windows are now what greet guests when they walk through the front door of the apartment.

Because the home benefits from 360-degree views of the city, the colors of San Francisco were the touchstone of the design scheme. What you see outside is reflected inside: the distinctive red of the Golden Gate Bridge, the reflected blue of the bay, and the golden glow of the city at night were all incorporated into the palette. The client requested a strictly traditional scheme for this pied-à-terre, but I made it my priority to layer comfort into their formal taste. Antique furniture and master paintings veil the softness of silk, cashmere, and velvet. Like a perfectly tailored suit, this apartment adheres strictly to the rules of design while managing to also be luxurious and comfortable.

Good hardware is the fine jewelry of a home. The gold octagonal door handles are from P. E. Guerin; their value comes from their functionality as much as their appearance. The Goyard umbrella stand was a present to the clients from me. They are from Southern California, and I thought they needed a new piece of furniture to help them adjust to the change in weather in the Bay Area.

ABOVE: In the entry hall, a seventeenth-century Russian burgundy glass pendant light drips with delicate crystals, and celadon ginger jars sit atop antique English oak pedestals. I wanted a very dramatic opening statement to this apartment that would befit the building's heritage, so I applied gold leaf to the walls and hand painted a de Gournay bamboo river blossom over the leafing.

OPPOSITE: I paneled the library in a warm caramel-colored walnut to create a stately backdrop for the clients' extraordinary collection of plein air paintings. The ottoman is upholstered in scraps of an old carpet.

PREVIOUS SPREAD: The living room had been completely gutted down to the studs, but the original plaster cornice from the 1920s was kept intact. The German baroque polychrome-painted carved-wood centurion is from the late seventeenth century. The industrial French painted-iron cabinet dates around the 1880s. The one hint of modernism in this space is the abstract painting on top of the cabinet.

ABOVE: I designed the sunroom as a space for intimate conversation, and it's equally (if not more) inviting when the sun goes down. To get a good look at the city, I found the most incredible antique telescope. Just add a cocktail and you've got the perfect after-dinner activity.

OPPOSITE: I opened up a poky old card room to give the living room a more modern scale, but I kept the concept alive by adding this small game table and chairs. It's an intimate pocket in this luxuriously sized room, and it is a great place to quietly take in the view.

ABOVE: I stained the oak cabinets of the bar an oxblood color and paired them with creamy-white marble countertops and backsplashes. It's a combination I'd not seen before, but the dramatic contrast works perfectly in a little room that only comes to life after the sun goes down. The clients' collection of plein air paintings is constantly expanding, and canvases show up in unexpected places all over the house.

OPPOSITE: I selected the French brass bamboo dining chairs from the 1950s for this very traditional room precisely because they are an unlikely choice. They lighten the decidedly formal mood given off by the deeply polished cabinet and table, the collection of antique boxes, the heavily carved architectural detail, and the rock-crystal chandelier.

ABOVE: In contrast to the dark wood found elsewhere, the kitchen is a placid, creamy space designed to take full advantage of the brilliant morning light. (The stone counters match those in the butler's pantry, providing unity between the two rooms.) The red and gold lantern from Charles Edwards in London is the star of this otherwise neutral room.

OPPOSITE: A small niche in the hallway is the perfect spot for this secretaire. The spectacular carved French mirror with its black lacquer border pairs beautifully with the ebony desk chair. The raw silk on the chair is exactly the same color as the paint trim on the walls. The walls are papered in a gold grass cloth that makes the entire hall glow.

ABOVE: Upholstering the walls in a bedroom is a wonderful way to control noise. Padded walls dull sounds from outside so you are guaranteed a quiet night. The walls in this bedroom are a very pale blue silk, and the drapes and carpet are silk too. An ornate carved eighteenth-century Venetian bench was the last piece I found, but it looks like the piece the entire room was built around. This was a good place to depart from the plein air collection, as the vibrant orange abstract painting provides some necessary frisson.

OPPOSITE: Countless yards of fabric and trim were employed in the draping of this hand-carved four-poster bed in an effort to make it a place you'd never want to leave. The room has a panoramic view of Alta Plaza Park and the San Francisco skyline. The walls were painted in a subtle strié, inspired by the delicate tone-on-tone stripe of the bed curtains. The bed curtains were made by Sherrie Horner, who was schooled in Paris. Her work is the haute couture of drapes. Hand-embroidered Irish linens encourage you to hit the snooze button one more time.

ABOVE: Installing a project is my favorite part of the process. I love seeing my vision come together in real life after up to three years of design work. The day the furniture finally goes into the house feels like the beginning of the last mile of a marathon.

OPPOSITE: Another bedroom with noise-cancelling upholstered walls, this time in a saturated red. I picked the color because the space is small enough to carry a bold color without being overpowered. To keep the red in line, I added cream bed linens and accents of varying shades of blue.

MORE OFTEN THAN NOT, IT TAKES SOME TIME FOR THE MEANING OF a home to reveal itself. But in the case of this house in Northern California wine country, the meaning was clear from the start. When I first saw the massive cement forms jutting into the landscape from my vantage point on the valley floor, I knew I had a formidable opponent. This home does not sit at the top of a hill; it bursts out from it. Designing it was truly an adventure, and the clients are two of the most fun people I've worked for. They are game for any idea, and this home clearly expresses their boldness, joie de vivre, and willingness to be playful. However, the heavy architectural masses and stark gray walls made an aggressive statement that was more like a design confrontation. They required furnishings that were strong and sculptural enough to hold their own in the cavernous spaces, but that would also reflect the warmth of the homeowners.

As I do with most of my projects, I took my design cues from the environment. An interesting thing about this dwelling is that despite its modern, rather conceptual design, it sits on eight acres of virgin terrain, complete with a natural spring and two accompanying ponds. Throughout the home, floor-to-ceiling windows slide away and disappear completely, opening it to the Sonoma landscape, which is an expansive brushstroke of grays, blues, and browns. Here, dry wood and rusted metal seem to be as commonplace as shrubs and trees. These components became my palette for color and material. My objective was to diminish the line between home and landscape until it was nearly impossible to tell whether you are inside or out. I punctuated the sculptural furnishings with pops of unexpected color, drawing on the feeling of being inside an art installation, because for me, this house is as much an experience as it is a place to live. It's the most unlikely country house, full of seeming contradictions, which, just like its owners, always make me smile.

I used my signature hand-painted fish on stone-colored Indian tea paper on the walls in this bathroom. The primitive Belgian bench was impossible to sit on so I made a seat cushion from petrol-colored mohair. The pillow is made from the backside of old rugs that have been stitched together. An industrial table constructed out of a reclaimed spring and new metal concertina hinges changes in height depending on what is placed on top of it.

ABOVE: Cement floors and a plastic rocking chair can survive all kinds of torture, including my two very wet dogs.

OPPOSITE: This enfilade of windows in the hallway makes such a dramatic architectural statement that I didn't want to interrupt the rhythm with anything too jarring. A pair of minimalist chairs adds a gentle sculptural touch to the room's starkness, and the David Michael Green sculpture introduces a burst of fiery gold to the gray expanse.

We inherited the massive sofas (which are made of rough-hewn tree trunks) when we started the design process—they were too heavy to move. A pair of Marco Zanuso armchairs has a funky retro quality; they are upholstered in leather in the most perfect shade of blue. The two heavy African cast-bronze tables are like a sculpture that you can rest your feet on. The glass vases are the same color as the chairs, a slight moment of matchiness that I could not resist. The spirit of the room is not at all serious— the ape sculpture above the sofa is a good tip-off, right?—so a little moment of twee matching is acceptable, I think.

ABOVE: The dining area is surrounded by sliding glass doors that slip away to reveal the deck, which has endless views of the wine country. This house is all about the dramatic interplay of simple shapes, which the relationship between the sleek brass Willy Rizzo dining chairs (upholstered in their original chocolate-brown suede) and the cone-shaped dining table underscores perfectly.

OPPOSITE: I set up an outdoor dining area right next to the pool, an arrangement I feel is conducive to easy entertaining. The woven rattan chairs are vintage French, and they don't try to compete with the terrific view. I positioned the sculpture, fondly known as *Hey Sheep*, by the pool to give the setup some humor. In a house whose design is dominated by harsh geometry and hundreds of tons of poured-in-place cement, a little whimsy goes a long way.

ABOVE: I took most of my design cues from the strong, stark look of the house, but there are limits to my obedience. A Regency-style tufted sofa upholstered in a waxed cotton by Coup d'Etat has no connection to the house's architectural style, which is exactly what made me want to use it here. I paired it with a patchwork rug from Mansour to prevent the composition from becoming too formal. I added two more African cast-bronze tables and a hand-carved wooden table to give this multireference design collage a passport to the aesthetic of the rest of the house.

OPPOSITE: The kitchen is an ode to the power of simple geometry: lines, squares, and rectangles. The penguin sculpture is by Seff Weidl, and the sculpture on the range countertop, which mimics the chunk of wood on the kitchen island, is by Minoru Ohira.

ABOVE: This eighteenth-century carved stone sink was the starting point for the design of the bathroom. To pair it, I took a quick cruise through the decades and came up with an ultra-modern Boffi faucet and an Italian mirror from the 1960s. The towels are by Nancy Stanley Waud, my go-to source, whose signature custom pieces help you remember what goes where.

RIGHT: The outdoor shower is shielded by a massive piece of bleached wood so the dogs can have some privacy.

OPPOSITE: The master bedroom is entirely encased in glass walls, which made for a fun exercise in reexamining the conventions of bedroom furniture. Without the usual wall to put the bed up against, I devised a scheme using an upholstered screen, which does double duty as a headboard easel. The brown velvet tufted chair can face into the room in the traditional way, or swivel out to take in the view of the countryside. The bed linens are custom-tailored by Holland & Sherry.

STEADY

The yearning to feel safe is part of human nature. When the world outside makes one feel constantly vulnerable on every level, what better provider of safety is there than a home? That essential feeling of refuge, what I call a "steady" environment, isn't created by the physical mass of furniture or the weight of the drapes. Rather, it comes from spaces that feel comfortable, honest, and dependable. The homes in this chapter all share a sense of serenity and welcome, and no matter how large or how grand, they still manage to feel cozy. Each of the homeowners has brought in the spirit of his or her family and traditions, and these personal connections are key in creating a meaningful, steadfast haven. I want every home I design to feel like a place where nothing can ever go wrong.

This bust is a flea-market find from Paris. I built a simple metal stand for it and placed both in the entry window. White linen drapes frame the sculpture and create a balanced composition. A custom appliqué on the drapes's leading edge adds a contemporary crispness.

Los Angeles
California

AFTER THE OPENING OF THE SANTA MONICA RESTAURANT, TAVERN, which my firm designed, my phone started ringing off the hook. All of a sudden, everybody in the Los Angeles area who was building or decorating a home wanted a house like that. One of the calls was from a delightful young couple with an expansive, classically American home located right up the street from mine. She wanted Tavern, and because I instantly liked her, I said that I would oblige, although I know that you cannot copy and paste a design scheme from one space to another. To create a home and produce a design that is meaningful and practical, you have to take into account the location, landscape, architecture, and, most importantly, who the clients are.

This scheme started as a balancing act between traditional architecture, the clients' existing antiques, and the couple's youthful disposition. I started with a much lighter palette than Tavern has to make the spaces feel airy and fresh. Then I incorporated cheeky pieces of art, a playful light, or in the case of the family room, a rug with my signature fish motif—a choice that reflects his sartorial taste and her softer side. I also wanted to make this a home that they could grow into, so I purposely "underdecorated," with an eye toward creating flexible spaces and easy designs that can naturally evolve. As time passes and their collections expand, the home can be emblematic of who they are as a family at each stage of their lives, and thus become increasingly meaningful to them as the years go on. She still jokes that she prefers Tavern, but now their friends call and ask me to copy their home.

One of my cardinal rules of design is to work with a good curtain maker. These simple white linen curtains are dressed up with a geometric appliqué in electric blue alpaca. A striking painting by Bo Joseph introduces a single splash of scarlet to the blue and white room. The walls are covered with a metallic-backed grass cloth so they shimmer and reflect the light as it changes throughout the day. A wrought-iron game table by Soane has a deep-blue leather top. The egg-shaped lamp is 1960s Italian.

ABOVE: I fell in love with the perfectly symmetrical façade of this house by the firm Thomas Proctor Architect. The creeping vine will one day cover the whole house—and I hope that my clients are still living here when that happens.

OPPOSITE: Gray silk lines the walls of the entry hall and tempers the sharpness of the white lacquer paneling. The ravishing red Swedish rococo grandfather clock is a beacon in a space otherwise ruled by grays and blues. The Gustavian bench is upholstered in a casual cream linen, but to balance that monotone, I covered the pillows in delicate silk and a leaf-patterned Fortuny cotton in silver and indigo. The striped chairs are family heirlooms, which desperately needed to be recovered when I got my hands on them. I picked a jovial stripe to make them feel more contemporary. I gilded the console from a Paris flea market in white gold to revive its character. The Ewerdt Hilgemann sculpture that sits on top adds one more modern note.

I am a true believer in the beauty
of unexpected geometry. This
octagonal library introduces a
surprising shape into this house,
which makes for a much more
interesting room than a standard
box but its strong symmetry
doesn't put it at odds with the
steady look of the rest of the
home. I was so smitten with
the angular organization of
this room that I was inspired
to continue the theme with the
bold geometric
appliqué I
used on the
drapes in
the living
and dining
rooms.

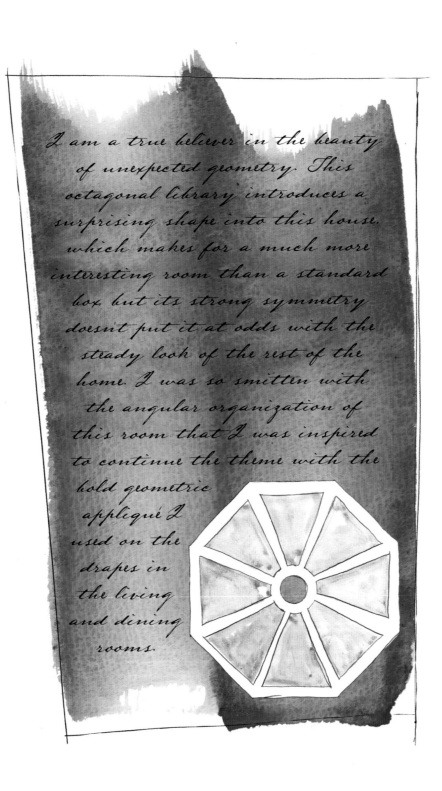

OPPOSITE: The octagonal library features a contemporary
Therien & Co. coffee table with a burled walnut top that appears
to float in the middle of the room. The sofa is upholstered in
de Le Cuona paisley. The coral stone lamp is 1970s Italian.

RIGHT: The sofas are my design for A. Rudin and are upholstered in a chalk stripe by Loro Piana. The horse painting is by Jane Rosen.

OVERLEAF: A pair of heirloom Chinese cabinets flanks a tufted sofa and showcases a collection of American ceramics from the 1960s and 1970s. To dilute the harshness of the black lacquer, I lightened up the interiors of the cabinets by upholstering them in pale blue cotton. The antique solid stone stools are from China; they help contextualize the Chinese cabinets.

ABOVE AND OPPOSITE: The table and chairs are family heirlooms. They were in perfect condition but felt a little staid so I brought them back to life by reupholstering them in lizard-green leather. The walls are lacquered blue and white, a color scheme that takes its cues from the artwork by James Nares. I added a daring Greek key–patterned rug and a graphic black-and-white photograph by Judy Pfaff to the mix. A contemporary light fixture by David Weeks is painted a custom dusty blue, and the parrot lamps are from the estate of Tony Duquette. A Clarke & Reilly hand-stitched bench helps to keep the room cozy. Too much leather and lacquer can be cold, so the upholstered bench also warms up the room.

ABOVE: This kitchen is all about graphic simplicity. White is the dominating feature, so black granite countertops and stainless-steel appliances add drama. The jam on the countertop (not to be confused with the JAM in the rest of the house!) is my mother's recipe. The leather and steel barstool is by Jim Zivic.

OPPOSITE: One of my favorite pieces of contemporary design is Lindsey Adelman's Knotty Bubbles chandelier of hand-blown glass and knotted rope. The massive primitive bowl is Belgian, and the metal bread trays are French.

ABOVE: The setup in the butler's pantry adheres to my rule that your home should always be ready for unexpected guests—especially ones that like a drink.

RIGHT: The design scheme in the family room plays it safe with a composed color palette of cool neutrals, laying the groundwork—literally—for the panache of the fish rug.

PREVIOUS SPREAD: These benches and campaign chairs are by Richard Wrightman. Three vintage American lead lanterns are aged to perfection. The organic shapes of the three coral stone planters soften the stiffness of the architecture and help make this alfresco dining area feel more casual—as it should be.

ABOVE: I am powerless to resist a good stripe, as this rug I designed illustrates. It casually subdues the ikat on the curtains and the bed.

OPPOSITE: This Art Deco French bar is inlaid with an unusual painted green metal; it houses a collection of handsome green glass demijohns. The sculptural bronze vase on top of the bar is by Richard Shapiro. The sofa is from my collection for A. Rudin.

ABOVE: A shower isn't the first place in which most people would think to set a Chinese garden seat, but I'm permanently wired to bring elements of real life into people's bathrooms. The steam shower is clad in slabs of Carrara marble.

OPPOSITE: Another vanity, another place for me to rebel. Rather than the traditional marble and tile, I covered this entire room in a dark-stained walnut—including the cabinets, the floors, the chair, an antique floor mirror, and a collection of brass-trimmed boxes. White Carrara marble counters match the shower, and the domed ceiling is painted a chalky white to bounce light into the room.

ABOVE: I took my decorating cues for this pool house from the color of the water. Pale powder-blue walls, blue-and-white striped lamps, and misty-blue chairs don't stray from the source. Punctuating the interplay between nature and man-made is the carved sculpture of interlocking wooden rings, which looks more like driftwood than art.

OPPOSITE: This arched picture window faces the ocean and has the most glorious views. To break up the vast swaths of white, I painted the ceiling a pale shade of green, upholstered the bench in a darker tone of the same color, and then positioned paintings and photographs around the tub. I love putting art in bathrooms; it makes a purposeful room feel more inviting.

Newport Beach
California

THE PROOF THAT THE MEANING OF HOME IS DIFFERENT FOR EVERY-body could not be better illustrated than in this residence. It is steps from the ocean in Newport Beach, and the sounds of crashing waves and seagulls can be heard from every room. But the pages that fol-low offer almost no clues to the house's seaside location. My clients wanted a formal and traditional home without beachy clichés. This time, I took my design cues from art instead of the environment. Their astonishing collection of plein air paintings (one of the larg-est in the world) was the most important part of the equation, and "elegant," "tailored," and "sophisticated" were the words that kept coming up in our early meetings. The romantic colors and deep im-pasto of the paintings became something of an obsession for me; every room was inspired by combinations I distilled from an endless collection of canvases. His passion for the paintings was so intense that it became infectious, and now I am a plein air junkie too.

The process of creating a well-appointed family home that just happens to be on the beach was challenging and edifying. The challenge in designing this home was incorporating a subtle con-geniality to a scheme that kept leaning toward stiffness. The clients have three children, two of whom were very young when we began construction. It was important for this to be a family home, and I just don't feel comfortable designing spaces that don't say in some way "people live here." Ultimately, we landed on a formal tone that is punctuated with hints of the ocean, and rooms that are stately but also tremendously comfortable. It may not look like dogs, cats, and children hang out in these rooms, but I can assure you they quite happily do.

Hovering above the Pacific Ocean, the master suite is a subdued space punctuated with bursts of coral. We didn't want to make any obvious beach-themed references, but the collection of seabird prints is a subtle reminder that the ocean is steps away.

ABOVE: I have never liked empty corridors. Hallways are
these interesting, intimate spaces, and most people will
spend as much time walking through their hallways as they
will sitting in their living rooms. To entertain the eye as you
walk from room to room, I insist on filling corridors up with
tables, chairs, art, and anything else I can lay my hands on.

OPPOSITE: We designed this library as much for entertaining as
for work—in its own way, a concession to the concept of a "vacation
home." A deep sofa and a pair of roomy armchairs are the perfect
spots in which to sip a scotch and talk politics, which the clients
love to do! A shapely desk floats in the middle of the room because
I tend not to like putting a desk against a wall. I intentionally chose
furniture that seemed too big for the room so as to replicate the
feeling of libraries I remember visiting in London, where space
is tight but the furnishings feel all the more comfortable for it.

ABOVE: The dining room walls are finished in Mandarin red with cream trim. Chairs are upholstered in one of my favorite Fortuny fabrics. The Dutch chandelier is reflected in an ornate hand-carved Italian mirror.

OPPOSITE: My favorite part of the house is the grand entry into the master bedroom. This intimate sitting room feels warm and cozy, and it is the perfect preamble to the expansive view you get when you enter the bedroom.

OVERLEAF: This living room may appear formal at first glance, but like everything I design, there's comfort stitched into every element. I stuffed a striped silk sofa almost to bursting with down filling so that you feel cocooned by softness when you sit in it. I chose to forego the traditional coffee table and instead filled the room with plenty of small side tables, to create a more relaxed, salon-style atmosphere for drinks and revelry.

The family room is one of
the more relaxed spots in
the house. I created a feeling
of leisure with a graphic
lattice rug that I designed
for this room. I often start
designing a room from the
floor up, because a rug can
easily dominate a space.
I also hide televisions in
cabinetry whenever possible;
the television in this room is
tucked above the fireplace.

ABOVE: Excellent bed linens are one of life's great luxuries. These are percale, which I prefer to sateen. The embroidered Greek key design is a classic that will never go out of style. The comforter and Euro shams are silk with little thread bows that have been applied by hand.

OPPOSITE: Cole & Son makes some of the finest wallpapers in the world. This hummingbird pattern is a favorite of mine when I decide to give the fish a break. The purple porcelain lamp is by New York–based ceramic artist and lighting designer Christopher Spitzmiller. The green velvet wing-back chair is from Coup d'Etat's collection of made-to-order furniture. This San Francisco shop is one of the best stores in America and a treasure trove for designers across the country.

ABOVE AND OPPOSITE: My clients spend a lot of time in Paris and wanted their bedroom to feel like a hotel suite in the Ritz. I obliged and added a touch of coral silk velvet to the neutral envelope of creams and blues to give them the Parisian bedroom of their dreams overlooking the Pacific Ocean.

ABOVE: The average person will spend a year and a half of his or her life in the bathroom. So it makes sense to me that bathrooms feel more like living spaces. Here, I placed a round table in the middle of the room to activate the otherwise useless space between the tub and the vanity. A bench from Therien & Co. is a useful piece on which to drop clothes or take a seat after using the steam shower.

OPPOSITE: When guests visit, they have their own well-stocked linen cabinet so that there is no need to ask for extra towels, sheets, or pillows.

BRAVE

I admire people who call me to design their homes with a vision of exactly what they want. These clients are always creative and well traveled, and often are involved in some kind of artistic career. When working with creative people, I tend to play editor, corralling their endless ideas and stitching them into a cohesive look. The greatest part of working with clients like this is that they aren't hindered by fear of others' opinions, and they don't hesitate to experiment in the design process. I love working with people who are brave like that, because they challenge me to explore new design ideas and open me up to unexpected influences. The homes in this chapter are all owned by powerful female creatives. Each lives by her own rules, and each space conveys an impressive yet personal sense of style, flair, and originality.

The hallways of this Edwardian London home are papered in a hand-painted floral by de Gournay. I got the inspiration to paint the surrounding inset panels to match different colors in the wallpaper from a Damien Hirst painting I saw at the Tate Modern.

THIS SPANISH-STYLE LOS ANGELES HOME IS A FEAST FOR THE EYE, and the vibrant final product is evidence of how contradiction can create harmony. Every piece of furniture and decorative element has its own individual character and style, so the game becomes finding the links between the different elements of each room. This home has furnishings that are both ultramodern and from the past, from the Art Deco period and from the 1970s—you name the style and it's probably somewhere in the house. This goes to show that limiting oneself to a single style, color, or period may feel safe but it's no way to stimulate creativity.

The homeowner has impeccable taste—she is an artist who finds beauty everywhere. It is a pleasure and a privilege to watch her think about design. She approaches the process with an artist's eye and finds links in places few people would imagine. What's more, she feels no compunction to adhere to anybody else's rules. She loves what she loves and wants it in her home. The rest be damned. The result is a home that is truly expressive, unique, fresh, and challenging—one that is special because it does not conform to the traditional design rules. Every piece is a work of art, chosen for its beauty, craftsmanship, quality, or for some other intangible reason. I think some people might not see a singularity of vision in such a varied and colorful space, but to me, the meaning of this home is so clear because it's honest, unaffected, and so much about the creative process itself. This house is a treasure chest of inspiring creativity that I never tire of looking at.

A drop-leaf table from the early 1900s
is set in front of a contemporary
painting by Takashi Murakami.

ABOVE: Crocodiles need to bask in the sun to regulate their body temperatures. This cement reptile may not have quite the same needs, but he looks right at home in this bright courtyard. The Walter Lamb chairs were salvaged from a sunken ship in Pearl Harbor.

OPPOSITE: I was besotted with this audacious Swedish Deco rug for years but could never find a client brave enough to commit to it. You could not pair this rug with anything less than an Yves Klein coffee table. I allowed the sofas to be a neutral color only so I could cover them with orange cashmere pillows, a tribal textile with a cowry shell trim, and a collection of vintage woven ombré pillows.

ABOVE: I love the combination of the technological motifs in the Takashi Murakami painting and the ornate carving of these antique chairs. Both are so detailed, but in different ways. Putting them together draws out the intricacies in each one's craft. The turquoise ceramic lamp is by Peter Lane from Gray Gallery.

OPPOSITE: Virtuoso furniture designer Paul Evans made a very limited number of these cast-bronze consoles in the 1970s. The rhythmic relief of the sculptural doors is underscored by placing it near this simple naive pipe chair.

Inspiration sometimes
comes from the strangest
sources. I can't explain why
wriggling crustaceans first
came to mind, but I find
their black-and-burnt-orange
dappled shells intoxicatingly
beautiful, and lobsters are
a perfect reference in a home
of fearless decorating. They
were the inspiration for
this modern kitchen, where
black marble walls and deep
walnut cabinets were hand
waxed to bring out
the natural carrot-colored
tones in the wood.

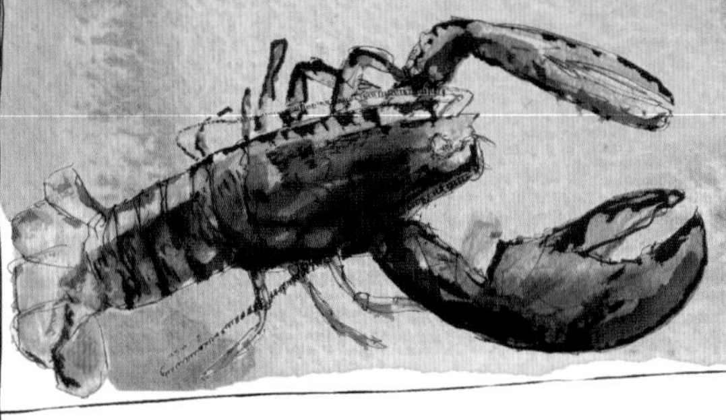

OPPOSITE: Even—or especially—in a home with such variety
in color and style, I stick with my credo that the simpler the
kitchen design, the better. The only ornament in this minimalist
space is a small bronze lamp shaped like a dog staring at an
illuminated ball. The sparseness of the design disguises complex
functionality—the ideal balance for a kitchen, in my opinion.

Dining rooms are much more exciting when you mix up different styles of chairs, but things really start to get fun when you throw in a bench. Here, I placed a Kaare Klint sofa opposite a bright assortment of chairs. A space used just for formal dining can feel a little wasteful in this day and age, so I like to create dining rooms that feel more multipurpose. With more comfortable, versatile furniture, this room can be anything from home office to library to part-time family room. (One member of the family has already cast his vote for dog kennel.) The slate and scarlet rug is by my friend Christopher Farr.

London
England

ACTRESS GILLIAN ANDERSON'S LONDON HOME IS A CATALOGUE OF her travels across the globe. She has an eye for the unusual and the offbeat—fitting for an actress who rose to fame on television's *The X-Files*. To complement her eccentric, globe-trotting taste, my business partner in London, Christine Kennedy, and I wanted to scour the most obscure vintage and antiques shops for surprising and unusual items. Fortunately, we were in Notting Hill, so we simply stepped out the front door of Gillian's house and headed to Pimlico Road, where eccentric decorative oddities are a specialty. We also found the best painters in London and put them to work lacquering walls in deep reds, layer upon layer until we all agreed on the perfect color, which was not an easy task. Then to make things more elaborate, we applied gold leaf to the doors and ceilings with the goal of enticing the eye to move from each shimmering room to the next. Dull gray London winters are no match for this fiery interior.

When it comes to the meaning of home, Gillian is the perfect example of someone whose environments always reveal a lot about her and how she lives. The many homes she has had over the years are like the multiple roles of an actress, each possessing an entirely different style and character that is in tune with each different setting. Yet Gillian also takes something from each place she lives in and brings it into the next, using one experience to inform the ones that follow, just like life. This home is the ultimate statement that expresses the personality of the owner while also saying something entirely new.

Lots Road Auctions in Chelsea is one of the best places to shop for vintage and one-of-a-kind pieces. The sofa and Abercorn Arms sign were purchased there. We covered the sofa in hot-pink linen. The walls are lacquered in a saturated red.

The doors to the living room were purchased
from a Moroccan importer. The opening had
to be increased to accommodate their height.
The sofas and tassel-trimmed chair were
found in Notting Hill. The artwork is a series of
wallpaper printing screens from Retrouvius,
which are backlit to expose the design. The
rug is from the Rug Company. Gillian found
the coffee table with its elephant and mahout
on one of her international adventures.

OPPOSITE: An antique chair, upholstered in lime-green toile de Jouy, was purchased in Notting Hill. The kooky painted coat is from Gillian's collection.

ABOVE: I like to put a little fun into every room I design, but this may have been the first time I literally brought in a carnival. The beaded headboard is made from part of an old carousel we found on Portobello Road. The worn leather bench at the foot of the bed was bought at a Lots Road auction, and we remade the seat cushion in plush velvet but kept the stuffing loose, as it had been originally. The walls are papered and block printed by hand. The ceiling and French doors are gold leaf. Curtains are blue velvet from Pierre Frey.

Los Angeles
California

WHEN YOU SPEND MUCH OF YOUR LIFE ON PLANES JETTING FROM one fashionable destination to the next, as our client and dear friend Amber Valletta does, you are bound to bring back inspiration from every place you go. Finding a balance between the worldly influences of high fashion and the desire to create a comfortable, intimate family home was the challenge for her Los Angeles abode. The most marked characteristic of Amber and her family is that they are wonderfully normal. They spend lots of time at their sons' hockey matches and at their second home in Oklahoma. The fast-paced glamour of Hollywood and Paris couture are only accents on a close-knit family dynamic.

During our initial discussions about renovating their home, I scribbled a floor plan on a napkin on the original kitchen island and said, "This is how you should live." That scribbled floor plan was the start of a completely new environment—and new way of living—for the family. I opened up the living spaces into an enfilade of rooms that family members could easily flow through. Elsewhere, I kept some secluded spaces, so each person could retreat to quiet corners when needed. Amber and Ross then took the reins in translating the floor plan into reality by incorporating earthy materials, unvarnished wood, honed stone, and handmade Moroccan tile. Then we layered in some glamour, with expressive colors and hand-painted wall coverings. Amber's main criterion was that everything has an artisanal quality, so we hunted for handmade pieces and worked with living artists. Amber's home is a testimony to how grounded and creative she is. It's a space that pulls off the neat trick of being both stylish and endearingly humble—just like her.

A Michael David Green driftwood sculpture sits atop a heavy stone table. Amber found four pewter legs on a trip to India, and we designed the bench that sits in the background by adding a blue suede tufted top. The photograph of the pigeon coop is by Amanda de Cadenet.

Denim-blue Indian tea paper lines the back wall of the family room. The ottoman was designed with Amber and is a testament to her bravery: we set it on fire to get the charred black base, and then upholstered it in simple purple linen. The wing-back chair is early 1900s English. A pair of blue Venini vases rests on a silver tray on the ottoman. We got the massive terra-cotta jar from an importer and turned it into a lamp.

Carrara marble frames a silver de Gournay wallpaper printed with delicate foliage. The dining table is Roche Bobois and the chairs are by Gervasoni. The bench was custom designed and upholstered in lilac calfskin. The blackened copper ginger jar is by Robert Kuo.

Not a single knob or pull is visible in Amber's kitchen; all the cabinets open with the lightest touch. The upper cabinets are my modern take on old-fashioned milk glass; they look as if they are painted on the back. Their sleek surfaces contrast with the warmth of the unvarnished walnut on the lower cabinets and the floors. A hand-blown glass vase by Jeff Zimmerman joins an eclectic collection of artwork by John Baldessari and Annie Leibovitz, among others.

PREVIOUS SPREAD: The library is a quiet retreat filled with mementoes from Amber's career in fashion. The room is lacquered in two shades of blue, and the books are organized by color. Art and photographs hung on the face of the shelving punctuate the columns with color. The ceiling is papered in handmade wallpaper painted with two colors of stripes, which exactly match the lacquered cabinets. The desk is from Hélène Aumont and the lamp is by David Linley of London.

RIGHT: Family photographs cover the back wall of the bedroom, along with works of art that have a personal significance to the couple. A rocking chair made from tree branches and twine adds a craftsman touch to the tailored space. The bedding includes vintage textiles and embroidered sheets that we had custom colored to match the walls.

Hot-pink grass cloth covers the walls of the master sitting room, while dreamy hand-painted abstractions by Kelly Porter flow across the ceiling. The daybed is Biedermeier and is from Amber's New York apartment. For this house, we upholstered it in a Turkish textile we found at a Paris flea market. The black lacquer chest of drawers is inlaid with a brass squid. The rug is by Christopher Farr, and the futuristic metal table is by Dutch design star Marcel Wanders.

South Kensington
London

IN LONDON, WHERE SPACE IS THE ULTIMATE LUXURY, IT'S A HAPPY day when you find a house with enough room to have some fun in. This extraordinary home in South Kensington has plenty of room—and a wonderful owner who gave us free rein to do whatever we wanted, so long as it wasn't beige. At the start, she handed me a pair of pink crocodile Dior stilettos and said, "Make my house look like these." In that instant, she threw down the gauntlet, and we had to turn an 1800s four-story Boltons house into something new and colorful.

Until our client bought it, the house had been in the same family since its construction. All of the original paneling and plasterwork were in need of restoration. To our advantage, there was something relaxed and almost casual about the interior architecture, which is a rarity in buildings designed centuries ago. And the house had exceptional bones, which thankfully could support our every whim. We updated the facilities but kept the original decorative details. I am a stickler for tradition and a firm believer that it's a crime to destroy good craftsmanship. We painstakingly restored every architectural detail and kept the floor plan true to the original.

The English are geniuses at combining ultramodern and Old World under one roof, a marriage that thrills me because it both honors tradition and encourages innovation. With the bones squarely in place, we added modernizing elements that went as far from the past as possible in order to make the house feel relevant for today's lifestyle. Then all that remained were the flourishes: flocked wallpaper, multicolored paneling, embroidered walls, and feathered chandeliers. A knight in shining armor completed the composition, a finishing touch that is equal parts folly and formality, and says everything you need to know about the meaning of this home.

This tiled alcove represents so many things that I adore about English design: a mixture of materials, the fearless application of pattern and color, maximizing function in small spaces, and incredible attention to architectural detail. All I did here to complete the look was add some fun owl andirons, a cheerful yellow French mattress, two hand-printed pillows, and a lot of elbow grease.

OPPOSITE: This home is located on the Boltons, a glorious treelined street in London's Royal Borough of Kensington and Chelsea. The redbrick and stone façades are emblematic of the architecture in London during the mid-nineteenth century.

ABOVE (LEFT and RIGHT): Bringing humor into decorating is essential in my opinion, so having a client with a sense a humor is a big plus for me. The foyer of this London home is guarded by a knight that was found at an antiques auction in Brighton, and it would not surprise me at all if my client hides inside it herself on occasion. The stairs are papered in de Gournay's iconic Chelsea design. We picked lemon yellow for the ground paper. The trees on the custom-printed wallpaper climb up all four stories of the house and spread into the hallways. This print references the trees that grow outside the window of this client's South Kensington neighborhood.

ABOVE AND OPPOSITE: Being fearless about color and pattern opens up a world of decorating opportunities. No one is better at mixing different looks than the English, and I completely embraced the lessons about this that I had learned from going to design school in London. I upholstered the walls of this family room in a colorful Chinese print, which I continued on the drapes.

ABOVE: Though we don't know who made this painting of wild horses, we chose it for the free spirit that it evokes. I don't believe a piece of art needs to be expensive or important to get a place on your walls. It can be just as interesting to display pieces that say something about (or to) the owner, regardless of monetary value.

RIGHT: The kitchen is übermodern, a departure from the wood paneling and stone edging in the rest of the house. The decision to go contemporary was based on function: the room is small and benefited from a modular German kitchen with a precision design that maximizes efficiency. So as not to lose the English thread entirely, we introduced a flocked patterned wallpaper by Cole & Son that was also used in the Houses of Parliament.

ABOVE AND OPPOSITE: Though it's been years since I designed this room, it never fails to excite me. In London, where the weather is often gray, I think it's important to create vibrant interiors that stave off dreariness. The walls are upholstered in the most incredible embroidered floral and trimmed in a ravishing fuchsia tape. I upholstered the sleigh bed in matching fuchsia leather. The drapes are a comparatively demure green check. Crisp white bed linens trimmed with delicate lace beg to be slept in. I don't subscribe to the notion you need to have a neutral, spalike room to get a good night's sleep. Bedrooms can be sexy, romantic, or playful—but never dull.

ABOVE: A backlit Italian mirror with delicate glass blossoms hangs on the wall above a collection of enamel figurines.

OPPOSITE: The dressing room walls are upholstered in a jazzy yellow-and-pink stripe. The ottoman is upholstered in a bold Clarence House–patterned woven fabric. Tim Dolby painted the striking mural on the dressing room cabinet doors. It is based on a scene from a Victorian postcard that my client treasured. The chandelier drips with crystals and feathered shades. The floors are carpeted in a deceptively neutral stripe that works with anything—including the walls.

AT EASE

I have been lucky to work with some of my clients on several different projects. It's wonderful when a successful working relationship develops into a friendship, which then informs a continuing, hopefully lifelong, relationship. I love interpreting different iterations of a family's personality into various kinds of homes. Usually, I design a client's primary residence first, then do his or her getaway space: the pied-à-terre, the beach house, or the weekend cottage. I always enjoy creating spaces for people I care about when the goal is to make them feel at ease. I love the spaces in this chapter because they are restful—simplicity and comfort rule the day. They are wonderful spaces for me to be creative in because the objective—leisure—is clear from the outset. Clarity is one of the best lessons I've learned in decorating. When you know where you are going right from the start, you tend to put a lot less stress on finding one right way to get there.

Zinc lanterns hung from low branches light the gravel pathway that leads to a private guest cottage in Laguna Beach.

Laguna Beach
California

THIS LAGUNA BEACH HOUSE IS A COLLECTION OF CARIBBEAN-STYLE cottages arranged on a cliff overlooking the ocean. Inside is an artful jumble of Staffordshire dogs, leather-bound books, and English linen upholstery. Because the client is more traditional than your average Laguna beach bum, we set out to evoke a dreamy, nineteenth-century British colonial atmosphere based on his and my mutual love of the interiors of the British Virgin Islands, Bermuda, and Mustique. This home turns the image of the sparse, modern beach house on its head with no shortage of collected curiosities. It's thrilling when people choose the less-expected route.

The owner is the consummate entertainer and a strict adherent to proper etiquette. His parties, which are regular occurrences, are always events, with hand-addressed invitations, multiple courses, signature cocktails, and glittering guest lists. There are enough extra bedrooms for guests who have had one too many to spend the night. Every aspect of this home was conceived to entertain either the eye or the imagination. From the pale pink living room, inspired by the beaches of Harbour Island, to the subtly monkey-themed guest cottage, we focused on the little details, the kind that may only become obvious after a couple of cocktails. The meaning of this home is all about spirited, yet comfortable, entertainment. It has an ambience that invites visitors to put their feet up and relax with a whiskey—so long as they are dressed in the appropriate dinner jacket.

The property has two guesthouses. The Monkey Cottage has a collection of fun monkey prints on the walls. The bedding fabric is printed with an old map. I made the bed high enough so that visitors can wake up and immediately take in the ocean view.

ABOVE (LEFT and RIGHT): The living room is a testimony to my client's affinity for England. When I remember decorating this room, I recall more discussions about what we took out than what we put in! Because the house is on the beach, the design process revolved around striking a balance between a rambling English style and Californian simplicity. The cabinetry is by Michael Carey. Further evidence of this client's passion for travel: a mix of celadon vases from China, an armoire from England, and a painted English bamboo table that we combined with overstuffed upholstered furniture, in the true British tradition.

OPPOSITE: The dining room walls are papered in the same straw grass cloth as in the living room, and the color scheme follows through to here. I can't resist an opportunity to mix up a dining room, so here I varied Bennison linen with leatherhead chairs to stop the room from feeling too repetitive.

ABOVE: This second guesthouse is called the Palm Cottage because of the palm-tree print of the drapes. We raised the beds so that guests can fit large suitcases in the oversized storage drawers underneath. As in the Monkey Cottage, the added height of the bed gives the guests a clear view of the ocean.

OPPOSITE: This tented outdoor dining room in the middle of the property serves as a gathering point in the evenings for alfresco dining. I turned a pair of bamboo pagoda birdcages into lanterns to create a focal point. The Chinese statue was found at J. F. Chen in Los Angeles.

OVERLEAF: The deck is a clue to the fact that this is not your average beach house. Instead of a typical blue-and-white ocean-inspired look, we upholstered black wicker furniture from Palecek in a wild mix of red, gray, black, and pink.

Hollywood Hills
California

IT IS NO SURPRISE THAT THE MEANING OF HOME CAN CHANGE FOR a person as he or she grows. My first home in Los Angeles was this Regency-style house in the Hollywood Hills. It was designed in 1936 by Leland Fuller, an art director for the movies and a self-taught architect. I fell in love with its unexpected mix of Hollywood Regency elegance and brisk, streamlined Art Moderne lines. At that time in my life, I wanted a large, gracious home where I could have big parties and guests could spread out in quiet corners all over the house. Catered dinner parties for fifty people were a common occurrence. I decorated the light-filled rooms in brilliant citrus colors and tried to make the space feel vibrant and glamorous.

Over time, I realized that the parties and constant revelry were not as exciting as I thought they would be, and what I really loved about the house was its view of the city. I soon realized I didn't need all the space or the endless slew of houseguests, so I promptly sold the property and moved to the beach. Downsizing was one of the best things I did, but it's important to say that I don't think my Hollywood house was a mistake. I learned a lot about the meaning of home from that house, and I carried aspects of its design to the beach house I live in now. In both homes, there are cushioned window seats to curl up in, an excess of pillows for comfort, and light-filled rooms that take advantage of the views. I was able to reuse most of the furniture by simply reupholstering it. Each home represents a particular time in my life and says something distinct about who I am.

I was going through an upholstery phase when I decorated this house. This room is so cavernous that I felt the need to fill it up with plush, comfortable seating to make the room more habitable. It is one of my favorite places in the house to gather, which is how I think every living room should make one feel.

OPPOSITE: I use a versatile, custom-striped runner in a multitude of color combinations for not only beach retreats but also formal houses like this one. It is also practical, as the stripes hide dirt. The skirted table picks up the orange tones of the runner. An enormous photograph of an urn by Karyn Millet is the focal point of the space.

ABOVE: Yellow suede chairs flank an ebonized game table with an inset leather top. Oh, and if you don't feel like playing chess, it's also a very romantic place for dinner.

Whenever I see a bay window, I want to build a window seat. By integrating seating in the window, you can really take in the view and feel as if you are a part of it, rather than just looking at it from across the room.

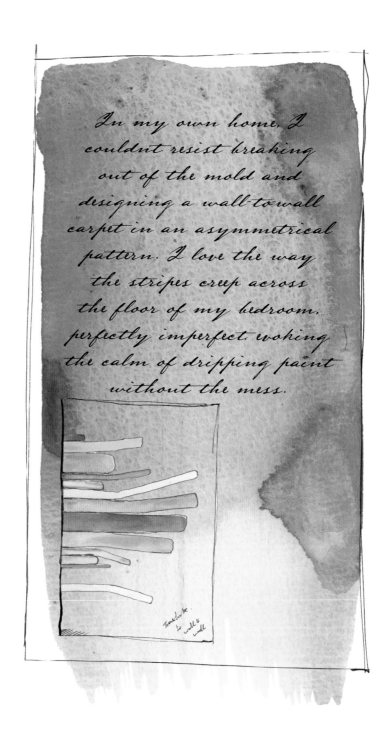

In my own home, I couldn't resist breaking out of the mold and designing a wall-to-wall carpet in an asymmetrical pattern. I love the way the stripes creep across the floor of my bedroom, perfectly imperfect, evoking the calm of dripping paint without the mess.

OPPOSITE: Whoever said wall-to-wall carpet needs to be one color never met me. I designed this one from a rug that I could not get in a large-enough size. The chair in the foreground is from my collection with A. Rudin; the deceptively simple design is extremely comfortable. The side table was found at an antiques store in Venice Beach. The peeling paint would drive a lot of people crazy, but I think that is precisely why it has charm—though it needs a visit from the Hoover almost daily.

Santa Monica Canyon
California

MY SANTA MONICA HOME IS ON THE SIDE OF A HILL OVERLOOKING the sea. Originally, there was a large piece of empty land on the property, on which I decided to build my own private work area. I flattened out part of the hillside, constructed a simple board-and-batten "shed," and turned it into a place to do a little work in, escape from Ross and the dogs for a bit, or just stare out the window and look at the sea all day if I choose. I've always liked the idea of secondary buildings away from a main house, where you can sneak away to have some uninterrupted peace and quiet. I furnished the space with some of my favorite things and created a sanctuary for myself surrounded by towering bamboo, a place that inspires my creativity. I designed my fabric collection in this room and wrote the bulk of this book within these four simple walls. There are no ringing phones and endless email chains here, just a big pair of barn doors that open onto the garden. I think that if you are not able to afford your entire dream home, why not first try to create your dream room? A small, perfect, meaningful space within a home makes all the difference, and if you are lucky, you can expand your vision over time.

While the furniture is valuable—a collection of antiques and industrial pieces—the structure itself is very humble. The floors are particleboard, one of the cheapest building materials available. I painted the whole place myself and in the process discovered that a) I'm not a very good painter and b) the somewhat shoddy paint job actually adds character to the space—a New York-penthouse-quality lacquer job just wouldn't do here. My shed brings great joy to my life, and as a result, adds another layer of meaning to our home.

Batty sculptor Ron Pippin imagined this strange bird that sits atop the desk in my office. The chair is part of a collection of antiques that once belonged to Rose Tarlow.

ABOVE: I have no idea where I found this old rusted locker, but I'll never forget buying the lamp. Ross and I got it in Sag Harbor and decided to walk it home, even though it is filled with cement. Carrying the heavy, rusted, spiked lamp made the journey feel like an eternity. Did I mention it was raining?

OPPOSITE: I designed the pendant lights. They are painted purple and hang from rope. The rug is a hair-on-hide patchwork from the Rug Company.

ABOVE (LEFT and RIGHT): The drafting table is vintage, and the antique cabinet is from Obsolete in Venice. I keep a small library of my favorite fabric samples in the shed to help me get inspired when I'm designing.

OPPOSITE: I bought a pair of these old factory-shelving units from a supplier of industrial seconds in downtown Los Angeles. They are wonderfully indestructible. My sconce design was inspired by the pendant lights—a simple rope wrapped around a hook.

Nantucket
Massachusetts

HOLIDAY HOMES ARE FUN TO DECORATE BECAUSE CLIENTS TEND to be less concerned with creating interiors that will impress others than focused on building environments that are relaxed, comfortable, and inviting. They consider how they want to use the house and what type of space will help them escape everyday life. I've found that my clients are more relaxed when creating their holiday homes, and this shows in the finished design schemes.

It should come as no surprise that most people prefer their second home to their main residence. This Nantucket home, located on Brant Point, is one such retreat. The clients have two other homes that are much more formal, and the budgets on those properties were far greater than for this summer sanctuary. The design brief dictated that the bulk of the furniture had to be purchased from catalogues. We had a budget that we could not deviate from and a limited amount of time to renovate and furnish so the house would be ready for summer. In addition, the *Million Dollar Decorators* crew filmed the entire process. Despite the myriad challenges, this was one of the most fun projects I've worked on. I got to flex my creative muscle and enjoyed making the most of the shopping limitations. While none of the furniture was custom-built—a big difference from most of my projects—we still ended up with a home that is stylish, artful, and fresh. Even though I was under intense pressure to finish this open-floor-plan home on a tight schedule, surrounded by the TV crew, I felt a surprising sense of ease. I think Nantucket is one of the most perfect spots in the country, and this Shingle-style house evokes what I love most about it: the distinct East Coast version of laid-back California attitude, without the strict formality often found in New England. Like the getaways my clients use it for, this home exudes the spirit of its owners during their most relaxed times.

Stark white walls are brought to life by the addition of battens placed at equal intervals. Painting the battens a slightly brighter white helps define them more clearly against the walls. The color difference is so subtle that it is almost imperceptible. The photograph above the desk is an aerial shot of the adjacent beach by Piero Fenci, who also made the sculpture.

PREVIOUS SPREAD: We elongated the living space during the renovation process, and then moved the door on the right to make the room symmetrical. I wanted it to feel like a modern take on board-and-batten. The red boat on the mantel was found at the Pier Antiques Show in New York, and the oil painting is from Saatchi Online—one of the best resources for original art at affordable prices. The old metal table lamp continues the cog motif of the massive mirrors above the doors. An antique red foghorn was found on the island, and the wonderful painted red chair is from Nantucket House Antiques. All the pillows are from One Kings Lane.

ABOVE: To make the bar shelving more interesting, I mixed in some found objects from the island—a ship painting from the 1800s, a photograph of whale teeth by David Halliday, a carving of a fish, and a collection of stone pestles—with everyday barware.

OPPOSITE: The whales, oars, terra-cotta pot, and Swiss army blanket covering the bench are all from Coastal Antiques. The blue-and-white zigzag directors chairs are unmistakably Missoni, which I love.

OPPOSITE: This humble painted chest of drawers was found at an antiques store on the island along with the striking blue Windsor chair. In a nice twist, the factory lamp has surprisingly feminine lines.

ABOVE: When we started the redesign of this home, I picked this bedroom for myself, and I'm pleased to hear that it continues to be referred to as "Jeffrey's room." The walls are painted blue, my favorite color, and the sheets are embroidered with—what else?—anchors. The gray cashmere blanket is another one of my obsessions. The French industrial cabinets and lamps were found at Coastal Antiques, a shop on the island. Kevin Paulsen painted the three pieces of art in the room. Though they are contemporary, they have a magical quality that makes them feel as if they are hundreds of years old.

ABOVE: An all-white bathroom can be a little bland, so we painted the exterior of the tub gray and the ceiling a bright blue. As always, I brought in some real furniture, like this hand-turned chair and the impala-antler table. I love these diminutive pieces here because though they would be lost elsewhere in the house, they are the perfect scale for this relatively compact room. The seat cushion is washable, which makes it more practical for a bathroom, and this little seating area also makes a great space for stacking towels.

OPPOSITE: Walls lined with dye-free grass cloth bestow natural warmth to the master bedroom. I wanted to make the room feel as if you were inside the famous Nantucket basket. I layered a punchy zigzag rug over a woven sisal, which matches the color and texture of the walls. The acrylic table is outfitted with rope handles, which add a fun, nautical flavor to this modern piece. I designed the bench and covered it in simple gray linen. Having a bench at the foot of a bed is a practical solution to covering the end of a bed that has no footboard.

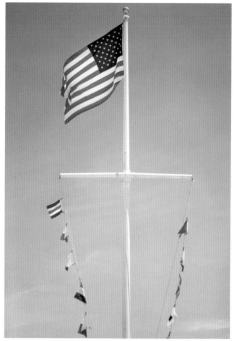

ABOVE (CLOCKWISE FROM TOP LEFT): These scenes of Nantucket exemplify classic, laid-back American style. Every building on the island seems to be clad in the same kind of gray shingles, and I find this uniformity breathtaking. There is an American flag on nearly every house—a patriotic touch I rather love. For me, the best pieces are usually discovered at the last minute. I pile up my finds in a Land Rover and drive them to the client's house myself. Here, we are making a delivery of an antique chair before heading to the beach for a spot of paddleboarding.

OPPOSITE: When renovating the property, we kept the original wide plank floorboards because we liked their generous width. Painting them gray instantly modernized the house. As anyone who has been to my house can tell you, I have a weakness for canoes in precarious-looking positions. I fell in love with this one at Nantucket House Antiques, and it just happened to be red and gray—the perfect shades for the house. This was one of those rare, lucky occasions when you find something so perfect for a home well into the design process that it feels as though it was made for you.

ACKNOWLEDGMENTS

WHAT I HAVE DONE IN MY LIFE IS POSSIBLE BECAUSE OF MY PARENTS. THANK you for giving me the freedom and encouragement to follow my passion.

Thank you, to my beloved clients Brett and Brooke Wyard, Jeff and Nancy Stack, David and Fredericka Middleton, Amber Valletta and Chip McCaw, Gillian Anderson, Caroline Styne, Suzanne Goin and David Lentz, Cynthia Cidre, Michael Lorber, Felicia and David Mandelbaum, Ben Bourgeois, Marjaneh and Dan Miller, Kelly Poe, Jillian Spaak, Solange and Herve Willems, Greg and Kathi Hansen, Mike Boone, and Dede and Klass Vlietstra, for allowing me into your homes and your lives. Without your patronage, none of this work would have been possible.

I'd also like to thank Caitlin Leffel and Suzanne Boone, for putting my thoughts into words; Douglas Friedman, who made shooting this book a joy—we laughed more than we photographed; all of the photographers who have captured my work on film over the years, in particular David and Ezster Matheson, Karyn Millet, and Grey Crawford; Margaret Russell, Michael Boodro, and Newell Turner, for making me a better decorator; the green thumbs of Scott Shrader and Michael Dilley, whose work is an inspiration; Michael Landrum, David Martin, Drex Patterson, Dwyer Maloney, Gep Durenberger, and Jeff and Cheryl Smith, who all have endless patience; Briony Newman, whose endless cups of tea and sympathy make life more bearable; my style council Diana Nathanson and Steven Gambrel, for your objective listening skills and incomparable hospitality; Danny Robinson and Barbara Vlietstra, for all of the heavy lifting; Meghan Day Healey, for the endless finishing touches; Tiffany Emerson, Lee Stanton, and Ray Azoulay, for always saying yes; Suzanne Rheinstein, for your gracious introduction to Sandra; Sandra Gilbert, for letting me do it the way I wanted and making it easy; Christine Kennedy, for believing in my work from the beginning and for telling me when it's all wrong; Keith Granet and Meg Talborg, for helping to make sense of it all; Jen Levy and Andy Cohen, for green-lighting me on the small screen; Jessica Debreceni, Giorgaina Magnolfi, and Brunello Cucinelli, for helping me always look the part; Eric Greenspan, for reading the fine print; Rob Yacullo and Forrest Wright, and Maurizio and Patritzia Petitbon, for your endless hospitality; Andrew Palecek and Ralph Rudin, for allowing everyone to have a piece of JAM in their homes; and all of my favorite dogs: Chessie Marks, Coal Cassidy-Marks, Foo Poe, and Roxy Shrader.

And most importantly, Ross Cassidy: Thank you for being the most understanding and patient partner and for putting up with me during the creation of this book.

RESOURCES

Antiques Furniture Lighting and Accessories

LOS ANGELES

Blend Interiors
blendinteriors.com

Brenda Antin
(310) 360-7500

Downtown
downtown20.net

Dragonette Ltd.
dragonetteltd.com

Galerie Half
galeriehalf.com

Habité Décoration
habitela.com

Hollyhock
hollyhockinc.com

Inner Gardens
innergardens.com

Kathryn M. Ireland
kathrynireland.com

Lee Stanton Antiques
leestanton.com

Nathan Turner
nathanturner.com

Nicky Rising, Ltd.
nickyrising.com

Obsolete
obsoleteinc.com

Mansour
mansourrug.com

Pat McGann
patmcganngallery.com

Paul Ferrante, Inc.
paulferrante.com

Peter Dunham Design
peterdunham.com

Reborn Antiques
rebornantiques.net

Therien & Co. Inc.
therien.com

NEW YORK CITY

Ann-Morris Antiques
annmorrisantiques.com

BAC
gallerybac.com

DeLorenzo Gallery
delorenzogallery.com

De Vera
deveraobjects.com

1stdibs NY
1stdibs.com

H. M. Luther
hmluther.com

John Robshaw Textiles
johnrobshaw.com

John Rosselli Antiques
johnrosselliantiques.com

Lars Bolander
larsbolander.com

Nancy Koltes
nancykoltes.com

Ritter Antik
ritterantik.com

Roarke New York
roarkenyc.com

Robert Stilin
robertstilin.com

R 20th Century
r20thcentury.com

Treillage, Ltd.
treillageonline.com

Wyeth Home
wyethome.com

SAN FRANCISCO

Coup d'Etat
coupdetatsf.com

Epoca
epocasf.com

Foster-Gwin, Inc.
fostergwin.com

Garden Court Antiques
gardencourtantiques.com

LONDON

Alfies Antique Market
alfiesantiques.com

Blanchard
jwblanchard.com

Carlton Hobbs
carltonhobbs.com

Charles Edwards Antiques
charlesedwards.com

Chelsea Gallery
chelsea-gallery.co.uk

Christopher Hodsoll, Ltd.
hodsoll.com

Guinevere
guinevere.co.uk

Heritage & Heritage Antique
Restoration
heritageantiquerestoration.
co.uk

Hill Farm Antiques
hillfarmantiques.co.uk

Howe
howelondon.com

Jamb, Ltd.
jamblimited.com

Jean Brown, Ltd.
jeanbrown.co.uk

John Nichola Antiques
johnnicholasantiques.com

Kenneth Harvey Antiques
kennethharvey.com

Lapicida
lapicida.com

Loveday Antiques London
lovedayantiques.co.uk

Phoenix Trading, Ltd.
phoenix-trading.co.uk

Pritchard Antiques, Ltd.
020 7352 6116

Retrouvius Reclamation
and Design
retrouvius.com

Robert Langford
robertlangford.co.uk

Rose Uniacke
roseuniacke.com

Soane Britain
soane.co.uk

Thomas Crabb Antiques
thomascrabbantiques.com

Vittorio Ragone
vittorioragone.com

Windsor House Antiques
windsorhouseantiques.co.uk

Fabric Houses Passementerie and Wall Coverings

Ashbury Hides
ashburyhides.com

Bennison Fabrics
bennisonfabrics.com

Clarence House
clarencehouse.com

Cole & Son
cole-and-son.com

Colefax and Fowler
colefax.com

Décor de Paris
decordeparis.com

Dedar
dedar-usa.com

De Gournay
degournay.com

DeLany & Long
delanyandlong.com

de Le Cuona
delecuona.com

Farrow & Ball
farrow-ball.com

Fortuny
fortuny.com

Fromental
fromental.co.uk

Gracie
graciestudio.com

Holland & Sherry
hollandandsherry.com

Houlès
houles.com

Janet Yonaty, Inc.
janetyonaty.com

Kravet
kravet.com

Loro Piana
loropiana.com

Phillip Jeffries Ltd.
phillipjeffries.com

Pierre Frey
pierrefrey.com

Porter Teleo
porterteleo.com

Robert Kime
robertkime.com

Rogers & Goffigon, Ltd.
(212) 888-3242

Rosemary Hallgarten
rosemaryhallgarten.com

Sandra Jordan
sandrajordan.com

Toyine Sellers
toyinesellers.com

Vanderhurd
vanderhurd.com

ADDITIONAL CAPTIONS

PAGE 1: My home is my laboratory, where I experiment with different arrangements regularly. I'm always trying to come up with fresh groupings of old and new furniture. The current iteration of the living room includes an antique wing-back chair and a canary-yellow tête-à-tête sofa of my own design. The bottle-green Hal side table was originally dark walnut, but it bored me so I had it refinished in a more lively verdant hue.

PAGE 2: For a New York City townhouse, I picked a subdued gray and blue palette to create a moody salon atmosphere. The bronze sculpture makes a dramatic statement against the cool walls. A table lamp in glazed ceramic by Svend Hammershøi for Kähler sits atop a leather and steel table by Jean-Michel Frank.

PAGE 4 (TOP ROW TO BOTTOM ROW, LEFT TO RIGHT): Gray and white are the colors I employed for this stately La Jolla living room; the bursts of pink from the upholstered bookcases pull you into the room. In a very traditional environment, the inclusion of one contemporary piece of art can make the difference between staid and fresh. A collection of marbled Nevada-wear ceramic vases, each unique, illustrates how groupings can make a strong impact. A leaded window from the late 1800s in a London townhouse. Every cook's dream is a well-stocked pantry; I put special thought into the design of this La Jolla pantry so everything stays organized. A family's collection of heirloom silver shimmers against chalky-blue shelves. Orange-and-white striped chairs welcome a reclaimed vintage door from Morocco to its new life in Texas.

PAGE 6: At Suzanne Goin's restaurant Tavern, I papered the walls in hand-painted silk by Fromental. The table base is an old factory cart from Germany. I used two pieces of reclaimed stone to make the tabletop. Flowers can make or break a room, and these peonies deliver a burst of color that is a signature of my work.

PAGE 9 (TOP ROW TO BOTTOM ROW, LEFT TO RIGHT): The farmers' market is a constant source of inspiration for my color stories. I find nature an endlessly imaginative resource. Suzanne's living room features a striped tête-à-tête sofa of my own design in front of a fireplace painted in Farrow & Ball Cooking Apple Green. In the library's reading corner, I've placed a comfortable French bérgère chair near the fireplace. A collection of books rests on a petrified-wood coffee table in the library. In the living room, a pair of wing-back chairs upholstered in stone blue mohair is welted in a jolly stripe to make them more playful. I chose zinc for the countertops in Suzanne's kitchen because of the way they weather. They are a good choice for a chef because they become more beautiful with frequent use. Cookbooks are never far from reach in Suzanne's dining room, thanks to the orange étagères, which were custom-made for the corners of the space. They also add a saturated burst of color against the subdued green walls.

PAGE 10: I've always had a fixation with everything nautical or boat related. I'm probably best known for the old rowboat that hangs from my bedroom ceiling. For a Nantucket beach home, I found this painted canoe. To me, it's a wonderful, sculptural piece.

PAGE 13 (TOP ROW TO BOTTOM ROW, LEFT TO RIGHT): A trio of Wilhelm Kage ceramic vessels rests on the Nero Marquina marble fireplace of a New York townhouse. My kitchen in Santa Monica has hand-waxed French oak cabinetry and an industrial-grade stainless-steel backsplash. The entry to Amber Valletta's home features wood-paneled walls, a primitive Belgian farm table, and an industrial sconce from an Italian factory. Cherry blossoms burst out of an old Chinese ginger jar for a dramatic centerpiece in a Beverly Hills living room. The red leather-bound books strewn across the coffee table echo the red tones in the Frits Henningsen chair. I designed the leather cabinet with nailhead trim in this cabana powder room as a place in which to hide laundry baskets. Relaxing on the beach in Nantucket, my favorite East Coast playground. A picnic in Solomeo, Brunello Cucinelli's village in Italy.

PAGE 14 (TOP ROW TO BOTTOM ROW, LEFT TO RIGHT): The intimate seating arrangement in this Los Angeles living room features a painting by Richard Serra and an Art Deco French tea table. The inspiration for the color scheme in this California kitchen came from the mottled black-and-orange shells of live lobsters, two of which are pictured here, in between a collection of glass jars. The three old leather chairs and the ornate bench by the fireplace in the courtyard of a Spanish Colonial home are unlikely choices for outdoor furniture, but they have both style and a sense of humor—the latter of which is an important aspect in all of my designs. This cavernous wine room was designed to be spacious enough to accommodate an expansive wine collection as well as seating for a dozen people—perfect for long, wine-centric dinner parties. A pair of carved-stone heads of mythical beasts merrily mingles with a painting by Retna, even though they were created about one hundred years apart. This simple outdoor seating area off the dining room of a Los Angeles home is livened up by one my favorite fabrics, a blue-and-white cabana stripe.

PAGE 220 (TOP ROW TO BOTTOM ROW, LEFT TO RIGHT): A French handle with a brass cap on the door of my private garden office. Rather than overfill a New York living room, I judiciously furnished the space with only the finest pieces of collector-quality furniture. Hard at work installing a Beverly Hills home. Industrial shelving showcases a collection of my favorite turquoise pottery in my Santa Monica Canyon garden shed. Ornate geometric carvings on a nineteenth-century Spanish cabinet. Poolside at a La Jolla home, where alfresco dining and entertaining are a year-round affair. Black lacquer cabinets, silver grass-cloth wallpaper, and a zebra rug frame an explosive, deep purple silk velvet settee.

PHOTOGRAPHY CREDITS

All photography by Douglas Friedman with the exception of the following images:

Ross Cassidy: pages 4 (middle row, center), 84, 141, 222 (middle row, left and right)
Jonn Coolidge: pages 196, 197, 198–9
Brunello Cucinelli: page 13 (bottom row, right)
Grey Crawford: pages 9 (top row, center; middle and bottom rows, right), 14 (middle row, left),
185, 187, 188, 189, 190, 191, 192–3, 195
Edward Duarte: pages 4 (middle row, right), 125, 127, 137
Marina Faust: pages 173, 175, 176, 177, 178, 179, 180, 181, 182, 183
Ed Golich: page 222 (bottom row, left)
David Matheson: pages 72, 73, 74–5, 76, 77, 80, 81, 82, 83, 135
Karyn Millet: pages 6, 9 (top row, right; middle row, left), 13 (middle row, center), 99, 106–7,
128, 136, 203, 204, 205, 206, 207, 220 (top row, left; middle row, center)
Briony Newman: page 172
Shelly Straziz: pages 13 (middle row, left), 159, 160–1
Elizabeth Zeschin: pages 153, 154–5, 156, 157

First published in the United States of America in 2013
by Rizzoli International Publications, Inc.
300 Park Avenue South
New York, New York 10010
www.rizzoliusa.com

Art direction and graphic design by Ross Cassidy
Production direction by Meghan Day Healey
Illustrations by Ross Cassidy

2013 2014 2015 2016 / 10 9 8 7 6 5 4 3 2 1

Printed in China

ISBN 13: 978-0-8478-4102-8

Library of Congress Control Number: 2013939438

Project Editor: Sandra Gilbert
Production: Colin Hough-Trapp